Railways & Recollect

Contents

Series Introduction

Railway publishing has been around almost as long as the railways themselves and there have been countless books with a historical theme, telling the story of a particular line, say, and occasionally linking the subject to its social context, but never before has there been, in such an accessible way, a juxtapositioning of photographic illustration of a railway subject with the events, happenings and highlights of a wider sphere and calendar. This series will, initially, take a particular year and place the views displayed alongside a carefully selected pot-pourri of what happened in that twelve-month period. The vast majority of the images in the first few books are from the Ray Ruffell collection, held by the publisher, but material from other sources will be interspersed where felt necessary

to maintain appropriate variety. Ray was a railwayman and photographer of equal merit and the main criterion for inclusion in these books is for the images to be both interesting and aesthetically pleasing within a chosen theme.

The books are aimed at a more general market than mere railway aficionados or enthusiasts and the series authors hope and trust that they will be sure in their aim and that you, the reader, will find much to enjoy, appreciate, enthuse about and even smile about! And it is hoped that some of your own memories are stirred along the way and that you may wish to share these with friends!

© Chris Harris 2008
Photos: © The NOSTALGIA Collection archive unless otherwise credited.

First published in 2008
ISBN 978 1 85794 296 5
Silver Link Publishing Ltd
The Trundle
Ringstead Road
Great Addington
Kettering
Northants NN14 4BW

Tel/Fax: 01536 330588
Email: sales@nostalgiacollection.com
Website: www.nostalgiacollection.com
British Library Cataloguing in Publication Data
A catalogue record for this book is available from the British Library.
Printed and bound in Czech Republic

Above: **GUILDFORD** Driver Bert Gabriel of Redhill shed has a twinkle in his eye, and a warm smile, having just arrived with the 11.05 Ex-Reading passenger service. His charge for this turn was 'Class U' 2-6-0 No 31619.

Frontispiece: **STOURTON DOWN**
A remarkable feature of the 1963 winter was that some of the heaviest snowfalls affected South West England. At Stourton Down, between Bridestowe and Okehampton, detachments of men from The Devon & Dorset Regiment and from The Royal Artillery Plymouth are seen clearing the line on Friday 8 February, following a blizzard on Tuesday 5 February that had resulted in drifts so deep that the 11.47am train from Plymouth to Exeter was snowed in from the Tuesday to the Friday. Many trains that normally took this route between Exeter and Plymouth were diverted via Newton Abbott, while passengers bound for stations on Dartmoor had emergency accommodation found for them by British Railways in Exeter.

Introduction

Nobody who experienced it will ever forget the new year of 1963. England was in the grip of the coldest winter since 1740, with most of the country blanketed in deep snow – which lasted until early March. The effects of these severe conditions, and the heroic efforts of transport staff to keep traffic moving, are well illustrated in this book. The writer must confess to having found that winter to be an enjoyable adventure, and remembers with pleasure several days when frozen or burst pipes resulted in his school being closed, thus freeing up another day for the much more enjoyable pursuits of riding around on trains or buses just for the fun of it – or to simply visit the railway or bus station, where the staff were always friendly.

Having at that time recently started to explore independently some of the delightful rural branch lines that then existed in Dorset and Hampshire, the publication of the Beeching Report on 27 March 1963 came as a great shock, and as the national railway network was subsequently reduced in size, perhaps in some ways nothing ever seemed quite the same again. In truth, of course, branch line closures had been taking place prior to the Beeching Report, but the whole process had now been given a new impetus and urgency and the list of services and stations proposed for closure made depressing reading. A number of routes were closed during 1963, including the branch from Radley to Abingdon, the line from Bewdley to Shrewsbury (in later years to re-open between Bewdley and Bridgnorth as the preserved Severn Valley Railway) and the rail link from Havant to Hayling Island among many

others. The Southern Region's third rail electrified network was not immune from closures, and 27 October 1963 was the last day that electric trains ran over the branch between Haywards Heath and Horsted Keynes, linking the preserved Bluebell Railway with the British Railways network (see page 29).

I could comment that the Beeching proposals felt like the great train robbery – but sadly that phrase was to be used in a more sinister context when thieves held up the Glasgow to London mail train on 8 August 1963 and made off with £2.5 million; the brutal treatment meted out by the gang to the innocent train driver was unpardonable.

In many ways it would be true to describe 1963 as a watershed year. The 1957 Defence White Paper had paved the way for the end of National Service and the last such conscript returned to civilian life on 7 May 1963. It was also the year in which the 'swinging sixties' really got under way and many previously entrenched attitudes were challenged. Looking back on 1963 in his anthology High Windows, published in 1974, Philip Larkin describes the year as the Annus Mirabilis, opining in the final verse of that poem that '...life was never better than in 1963 ...'. The old order was certainly changing; Private Eye (first published in 1961) and That Was The Week That Was (first seen on television in 1962) exposed the British way of life to a measure of satirical scrutiny not previously known.

It was during the spring of 1963 that the so-called Profumo Affair became public. This resulted in John Profumo, Secretary of State for War in the Cabinet, resigning on 5 June 1963 after admitting that he had lied to the House of Commons about a brief affair he had with the beautiful 19 year

old Christine Keeler two years earlier in 1961 – at the same time as Christine was also keeping company with a Soviet attaché, Eugene Ivanov. The subsequent publicity included the publication of one of the most iconic photographs of the 1960s, showing Christine on a chair of very contemporary design. In the wake of the furore, the Prime Minster, Harold Macmillan, resigned to be replaced by Sir Alec Douglas Home.

On the popular music scene times were changing too. Groups were starting to dominate the charts – the Beatles, for example, had three number one hits in 1963 (see page 42).

Times were changing in America also. It was at a demonstration attended by more than 250,000 people near the Lincoln memorial in Washington that Baptist minister Dr. Martin Luther King made his famous 'I have a dream' speech that has been credited with hastening the passage of the Civil Rights Act the following year. The assassination of U S President John F Kennedy in Dallas, Texas, on 22 November 1963 brought the year to an end on a more sombre note. Captioning Ray Ruffell's excellent photographs has brought back many happy memories for me; I hope you also will enjoy Railways and Recollections, 1963.

Chris Harris, Poole, Dorset, February 2008.

Background **SCOTTISH HIGHLANDS:** View from on board the Glasgow to Fort William and Mallaig express. Evidence of track maintenance being underway, a most uninviting prospect for the permanent way gang at such an inhospitable location should inclement weather set in!

Left: **DEEPDENE** On the morning of Tuesday 8 January, 'Class U' 2-6-0 No 31638 was pulling away from snow covered Deepdene with the 8.20am Reading to Redhill passenger train when Ray Ruffell took this photograph from the footplate showing 'Class N' 2-6-0 No 31830 roaring down the bank with the 9.05am Redhill to Reading freight.

Right: **REDHILL** Later that day, BR Standard 'Class 4' 2-6-4T No 80015 is seen departing from Redhill with the 10.11am service to Tonbridge. Local passenger trains between Reading, Redhill and Tonbridge were slated for withdrawal in the Beeching report, published in March 1963. Fortunately the service was reprieved, and was given a new lease of life from January 1965. Six special diesel electric units were provided for the route, each three car train consisting of two narrow bodied carriages from disbanded Hastings line units plus a normal width former 2EPB driving trailer coach. These unusual units quickly became known as 'Tadpoles'!

The Bleak Winter of 1963
'The Big Freeze'

Left: **OKEHAMPTON** Battle of Britain 'Pacific' No 34074 *46 Squadron* is seen shunting amid the packed snow and ice at Okehampton on Friday 8 February 1963. Built in 1946, *46 Squadron* looks in fine fettle in this photograph, but was withdrawn from service later in 1963.

The enormity of the task of clearing the line across Dartmoor is well illustrated by the main photograph. It must be remembered that apart from snowploughs fitted to locomotives, as here with 'Class Q' 0-6-0 No 30530, [*below*]

there was no modern state of the art snow clearing equipment in 1963. Where drifts were too deep for a snowplough fitted locomotive to force its way through, the clearance work had to be done by men with shovels. Transport staff are dedicated and industrious, and with help from the Army the West Country railwaymen cheerfully set about clearing the line across Dartmoor. Sadly this section of line between Okehampton and Bere Alston was closed just over five years later in May 1968, thus severing the former LSWR route between Exeter and Plymouth.

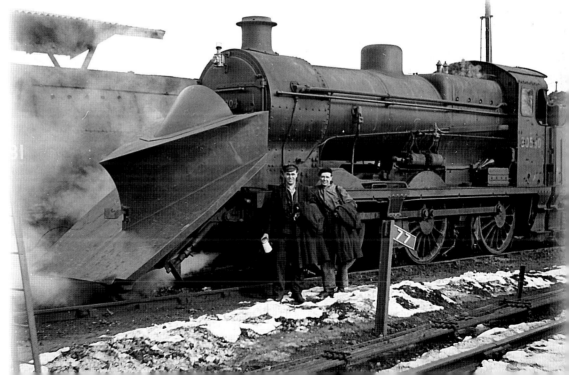

1963
Happenings (1)

January
England suffers the coldest winter since 1740.
Hugh Gaitskell, leader of the Labour Party, died.
General De Gaulle vetoes UK entry into the Common Market (EEC).

February
Harold Wilson becomes leader of the Labour Party.

March
Publication of the infamous 'Beeching Report' on the future of British Railways

April
Princess Alexandra marries Angus Ogilvy at Westminster Abbey.

June
Pope John XXIII dies, Pope Paul VI instituted.
John Profumo, Secretary of State for War, resigns over affair with Christine Keeler.

August
UK, US & Russia sign a partial nuclear test ban treaty in Moscow.
'Great Train Robbery'; £2.5 million stolen from a Glasgow – London mail train in Buckinghamshire.
Dr. Martin Luther King makes 'I have a dream' speech in Washington

The 1962/63 winter was recorded as being the coldest over England and Wales since 1740. Christmas 1962 was a very seasonable one, with Glasgow enjoying its first white Christmas for 25 years while Boxing Day saw the first snowfall of the winter across much of Southern England. This was just a foretaste of what was to come. During the early hours of Sunday 30 December 1962 a severe blizzard swept across the South of England and South Wales, with gale force winds causing considerable drifting. This was followed by a long period during which the daytime temperatures rarely rose above freezing point and the nights were bitterly cold; a minimum of zero Fahrenheit being recorded on one night in Kent. Despite drifts as deep as 12 feet between Tavistock and Lydford in Devon, the line was cleared by dedicated railwaymen and the train service was restored on Wednesday 2 January 1963. A further blizzard on Wednesday 9 January 1963 again blocked the line; the drifts were so deep that soldiers helping to clear an isolated section even attempted to blow a path through the

snow with explosives, but with little success. It was not until Tuesday 15 January that the line was able to reopen. Yet another blizzard with a force 9 gale on Tuesday 5 February brought drifts up to 20 feet deep, closing the line again until the end of that week while men battled to dig out stranded trains. Lying snow lasted well into March 1963. Another view of a snow clearance party, determinedly going about their seemingly endless task, is seen *below left*.

Below: **MAERDY** The bleak terminus at Maerdy was at the end of a branch from Porth on the former Taff Vale Railway in South Wales, and was part of the Western Region of British Railways when this photograph was taken on Saturday 23 February. The three car diesel multiple unit bound for Porth was built by British Railways Derby Works in 1957; the

motor open second nearest the camera had seats for 95 passengers. Sadly the three coach train appears to be well over capacity for the traffic on offer, and the branch between Maerdy and Porth was closed to passengers on 15 June 1964. Notice the coal trucks just visible in the sidings on the left.

Below: **ABERFELDY** A feature of the 1963 winter was the severity of the weather in Southern England, but Scotland also endured an exceptionally cold winter that year as seen in the photograph below. Conditions were starting to return to normal by early March, but the severe weather was not entirely over. It was freezing hard on the morning of 4 March when Ray Ruffell took this photograph of D5128 with the branch train at Aberfeldy. Hauling a train consisting of two modern BR Standard Mark 1 carriages, D5128 was built in 1958 and had a six cylinder Sulzer diesel engine of 1,160bhp. Aberfeldy was the terminus of a short branch that left the former Highland Railway route

from Perth to Inverness at Ballinluig; the branch closed to passengers on 3 May 1965.

Opposite: **NORTH BERWICK** The bitter winter conditions seen at Aberfeldy can be contrasted with the view opposite, taken at North Berwick on the warm and sunny 5 June. Headed by motor brake second No SC51124

built by the Gloucester Railway Carriage and Waggon Company in 1958, a two car diesel multiple unit waits for passengers at this delightful terminus at the end of a four mile long branch from Drem on the East Coast Main Line. Happily the North Berwick branch is still open in 2007, with a regular train service to and from Edinburgh.

Across the border to Bonnie Scotland

Writing of his travels on the former LSWR route from Waterloo to North Cornwall, John Betjeman spoke of the remoteness of the Atlantic Coast and expressed his wonder that the carriage he was riding in had started its journey in London. An even more evocative and romantic railway journey from London is to go to bed in a comfortable sleeping carriage as the train slips northwards through the suburbs, waking up in Scotland to partake of breakfast as the train makes its way along a single track line through stunning scenery. A type 2 diesel heads a train consisting mostly of BR Standard Mark I stock with flanges squealing around the curves on a summer morning in 1963. Notice the sleeping carriage marshalled next to the buffet car; the sleeper would have started from London the previous evening. The musical heritage of Scotland is rich and varied. Travelling by train through some of that country's beautiful scenery I am often reminded of the highly descriptive concert overture The Land of the Mountain and Flood, composed by Hamish MacCunn at the age of 19 in 1887. MacCunn was one of the first students at the Royal College of Music under Parry and this concert overture was very popular in its time; it is rarely played nowadays, although it did enjoy a brief return to popularity in the 1970s when a section was used as the signature tune for the television series Sutherland's Law. Sadly MacCunn died in 1916, aged only 29.

The year 1963 was a sad one for those who enjoy Scottish vocal music. Serious injuries sustained in an accident ended the singing career of Robert Wilson. Born in 1907 and initially trained as a draughtsman, Robert Wilson's fine tenor voice soon led him into amateur concerts, and he turned professional in 1930. For over 30 years he performed to packed houses all over Scotland, with radio and later television broadcasts bringing fame across the United Kingdom. He died in September 1964, having never fully recovered from his 1963 accident.

It is pleasing that in 2008 it is still possible to travel overnight from London to the Scottish Highlands, using First Scotrail's Caledonian Sleepers

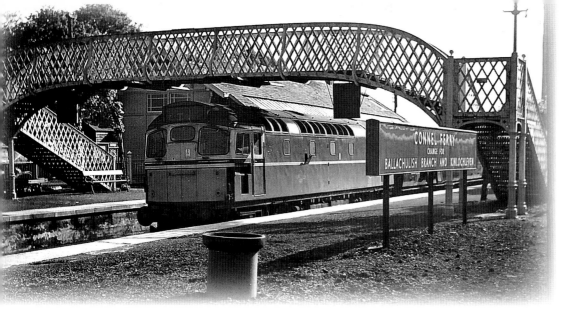

Below: **NORTH CONNEL** Also on 29 May, this photograph was taken from the train at the first station on the Ballachulish branch, North Connel. The view looks back towards Connel Ferry Junction and shows the structure of Connel Bridge in the background. This carried the branch over Loch Etive. At low tide the water recedes so fast from this sea loch that this area is known as the Falls of Lora. Work began on the bridge in 1898, with cantilevers from each shore giving a headroom of 50 feet above normal high water. At the time the only larger bridge of this type was the Forth Railway Bridge. After the branch was closed in 1966 the bridge continued in use as a road and in 2008 forms part of the A828; traffic lights control the flow of vehicles along the narrow single track road across the bridge. Notice the rudimentary buildings and the timber platform of North Connel station on the left; in contrast the name-board is a modern British Railways standard type which, in Scottish Region light blue, would have been only a few years old in 1963.

Above: **CONNEL FERRY** The station at Connel Ferry was opened on 1 July 1880 with the section of railway between Dalmally and Oban. The station was considerably enlarged when the branch to Ballachulish was opened in 1903; this rebuilding gave the station five platform faces – three through platforms and a bay at each end. Most trains for the Ballachulish branch originated at Oban, and therefore had to reverse at Connel Ferry to reach the branch line at Connel Ferry Junction which was to the west of the station. With hauled trains rather than multiple units this meant that the locomotive had to change ends of the train. On 29 May D5360, a type 2 diesel locomotive built by the Birmingham Railway Carriage and Wagon Company in 1958 is seen at Connel Ferry with the first morning train to Ballachulish. Following the closure of the Ballachulish branch in 1966 Connel Ferry station was reduced to a single through platform, but remains open in 2008 served by trains between Oban and Glasgow.

The name Ballachulish means settlement on the strait and this refers to Patrick's Narrows at the mouth of Loch Leven. The village has a dramatic location at the gateway to Glencoe, and some of the awe inspiring scenery is captured in this photograph of the 8.25am train from Oban after arrival at Ballachulish on 29 May. Notice the crossover that allows the locomotive to run round the train. Parcels are being unloaded, but there is little evidence of passenger traffic. Nonetheless it was a sad blow to many living in the scattered communities along this line when closure came on 28 March 1966. The station at Ballachulish was subsequently used as a garage for a time, and was later converted to become a doctor's surgery.

Above and right: **BALLACHULISH** For many years the principal industry at Ballachulish was quarrying for slate. Wagons in the goods yard and a loading crane can be seen to the right of the station name-board in this photograph taken on 29 May. A goods line continued from the yard to the slate quarries, which in turn were served by their own narrow gauge lines. The roof of Ballachulish locomotive shed can be seen behind the crane, while a water tank (steam locomotives for the use of) can be seen on the extreme left of the photograph. Notice how the station name-board has been economically mounted on old rails. Even in the early 1960s the slate quarries in the area were in decline, and in 2008 the principal industry at Ballachulish is tourism.

THE LOCH TAY BRANCH The five mile branch line from Killin Junction to Loch Tay was opened on 1 April 1877; there was one intermediate station at Killin, four miles from Killin Junction. Loch Tay station was closed to passengers from 9 September 1939, but this final mile of railway was retained because the single road engine shed was at the end of the line, a short distance beyond Loch Tay station. These photographs capture the flavour of the branch on 29 May, when the service was headed by BR Standard 'Class 4' 2-6-4 tank No 80093. Shown opposite is the small shed at Loch Tay, with [inset] the crew taking a break after coaling their locomotive. Loch Tay station is seen [right] still extant despite having been closed to passengers for over 23 years. The photograph [below left] shows the 7.05pm train to Killin Junction awaiting departure from Killin station, while [below right] we see the view from the footplate as the locomotive passes along the single track line.

Together with the line from Crianlarich to Callander, it was planned to withdraw passenger services between Killin Junction and Killin from 1 November 1965, but a landslip at Glen Ogle resulted in these services being withdrawn from 29 September 1965 without reinstatement.

Right: **EDINBURGH** Possibly the most famous of all British steam locomotive types were the 'A4 Pacifics' built by the LNER at Doncaster Works and designed by Sir Nigel Gresley. 35 of these distinctive streamlined locomotives were built between 1935 and 1938 and the type became the mainstay of express work on the East Coast Main Line between London, Newcastle and Edinburgh until ousted by the Deltic diesels in the early 1960s [see opposite]. A number of the class then worked for a few more years on the Scottish Region. 'A4' No 60016 *Silver King* is seen at Edinburgh Waverley on 4 March; this locomotive was in service from 30 November 1935 until 31 March 1965. Sister locomotive *Mallard* attained the world speed record for a steam locomotive in 1938, travelling at 126mph. The last British Railways service train hauled by an 'A4' Pacific ran between Aberdeen and Glasgow on 14 September 1966.

Opposite: **LONDON** Kings Cross is the London terminus of the East Coast route between England and Scotland, and is the location of this photograph taken on Saturday 25 May. By that date trains to Newcastle and Edinburgh were almost entirely in the hands of the very capable stud of 22 Deltic locomotives; an unidentified member of the class is seen at the head of The Flying Scotsman. More interest is being attracted by 'Class A1' 4-6-2 Pacific locomotive No 60133 *Pommern*, which is at the head of the White Rose express. Built to the design of A H Peppercorn, 49 of these

locomotives were ordered by the LNER but built under the auspices of the nationalised British Railways. *Pommern* was built in October 1948 and withdrawn in June 1965. The last of the Peppercorn 'A1 Pacifics' was taken out of service in 1966.

Above: **OBAN** The 12.05pm train to Glasgow is ready to leave Oban double headed by diesels D5360 and D5362 on 1 June. Notice McCaig's folly on the skyline. This was built on the instruction of local banker John Stuart McCaig during the last years of the 19th century to provide work for unemployed stonemasons; unfortunately McCaig died before the project was complete and the part-built structure has dominated the town for over 100 years.

Opposite insets: **AYR** When Ray Ruffell visited the Motive Power Depot at Ayr on 7 June, he was able to photograph an interesting variety of locomotives ranging from ex-Caledonian Railway 0-4-4 tank locomotive No 55264 that was stored awaiting the breaker's torch to 'Class B1' 4-6-0 No 61134 awaiting the next call to duty. Of particular interest is former North British Railway 'Class J37' 0-6-0 No 64541 [*centre inset opposite*] designed by W P Reid and introduced in 1914. Steam locomotives worked from Ayr Depot, which is joined to the running lines at Newton Junction and Hawkhill Junction, until October 1966.

1963 Arrivals & Departures

Births

James May	Journalist	16 January
Ian Cook	Footballer	18 January
Andrew Ridgely	Musician	26 January
George Monbiot	Journalist	27 January
Martin Bashir	Journalist	29 January
Jerome Flynn	Actor	16 March
David Thewlis	Actor	20 March
Julian Lennon	Musician	8 April
Natasha Richardson	Actress	11 May
Jason Isaacs	Actor	6 June
George Michael	Musician	25 June
Tracey Emin	Artist	3 July
Fatboy Slim (Norman Cook)	Musician	31 July
Tamsin Archer	Musician	3 August
Jarvis Cocker	Musician	19 September
Rick Allen	Musician	1 November
Lena Zavaroni (d.1999)	Musician	4 November
Nicolette Sheridan	Actress	21 November
Eddie 'The Eagle' Edwards	Ski Jumper	5 December

Deaths

Edward Titchmarsh	Mathematician	(b.1899)	18 January
Hugh Gaitskell	Politician	(b.1906)	18 January
J C Powys	Writer	(b.1872)	17 June
Guy Burgess	Double Agent	(b.1911)	30 August
Peter Craven	Motorcycle Racer	(b.1934)	20 September
Aldous Huxley	Writer	(b.1894)	22 November
C S Lewis	Writer	(b.1898)	22 November
John F Kennedy	US President	(b.1917)	22 November

Opposite main picture: **CARSTAIRS** Moving on to Carstairs Ex-Caledonian 4-4-0's Nos 54463 and 54502 are seen on 7 June in the company of a stored snow plough, which would have seen much use earlier in the year!

Above: **KILLIN JUNCTION** This lonely outpost is on the line between Crianlarich and Callandar and photographed on 29 May looking towards Glen Ogle and Dunblane. The branch to Killin and Loch Tay can be seen dropping away to the left beside the signal box [see pages 16 & 17]. The route from Crianlarich to Callandar, together with the Killin branch, was scheduled for closure in November 1965, but on 27 September 1965 a rock-fall blocked the line at Glen Ogle, and in view of the high cost of clearing the line the affected services were withdrawn immediately. A story, possibly apocryphal, is told of a local clergyman who maintained that the rock-fall was being used as an excuse to thwart a campaign by local people to keep the line open; he declared that the line could be cleared for £100. It is said that he was taken to the site on a wet day and offered a shovel by a British Railways engineer, who said that he personally would give the clergyman £100 if he could clear the blockage!

Above: **CALLANDAR** This tragi-comedy was in the future when Ray Ruffell took this classic photograph looking from the footbridge at Callandar as the crew prepare to depart, with a bright fire in No 45127's firebox, for the onward journey.

Catch It While you can...

A branch line just over 9 miles long was opened from Bere Alston (on the LSWR route between Plymouth and Okehampton) to Callington in 1908, although much of the formation had previously carried a narrow gauge mineral railway that had been built during the 19th century to serve the many mines and quarries in the area.

On 18 April 'Class 2' 2-6-2T locomotive No 41316 is seen at the attractive little terminus at Callington with the 9.45am train to Bere Alston. Manufactured at British Railways Crewe Works in 1952 and allocated to the Southern Region from new, No 41316 was built to a design by George Ivatt first

introduced in 1946 for the LMS. Not being push-pull fitted, the locomotive had worked the 8.24am service from Bere Alston to Callington tender first; the train consisted of two Maunsell carriages and a van [bottom right].

From 7 November 1966 the branch was truncated to run between Bere Alston and Gunnislake only. Following closure of the former LSWR main line between Bere Alston and Okehampton in 1968, trains have run through to and from Plymouth, reversing at

Bere Alston. Freight was still important on the branch in 1963; another 'Class 2' tank loco is seen [below] on a freight working at Callington, also on 18 April that year.

Callington

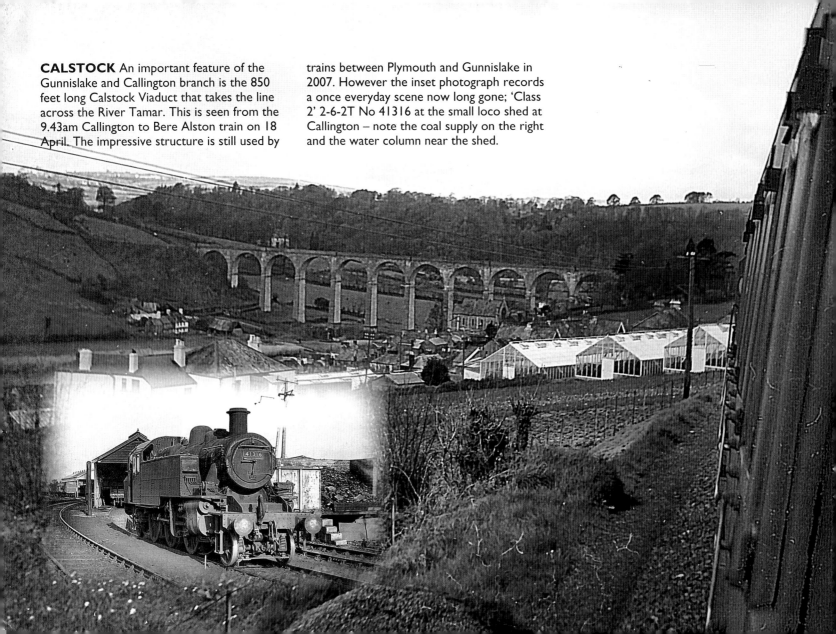

CALSTOCK An important feature of the Gunnislake and Callington branch is the 850 feet long Calstock Viaduct that takes the line across the River Tamar. This is seen from the 9.43am Callington to Bere Alston train on 18 April. The impressive structure is still used by trains between Plymouth and Gunnislake in 2007. However the inset photograph records a once everyday scene now long gone; 'Class 2' 2-6-2T No 41316 at the small loco shed at Callington – note the coal supply on the right and the water column near the shed.

The Railway Enthusiasts Club's Rambling Rose rail tour took place on 23 March 1963. Starting and ending at Farnborough, the route took in an interesting selection of railway byways not normally served by passenger trains as well as including sections of main line running. The route and booked timings are tabulated on the next page; it is unfortunate that a derailment at Whitchurch Town caused the train to run via the main line through Winchester City and Micheldever rather than as originally planned via Winchester Chesil and Newbury between Southampton and Reading. Motive power was provided by 'Class M7' 0-4-4T locomotive No 30108. The LSWR built 105 tank engines of the 'M7 Class' between 1897 and 1911, the vast majority at the Company's own works at Nine Elms, although the final 10 were constructed at Eastleigh. No 30108 was built at Nine Elms in 1904, fitted for push-pull working in 1930 and remained in service with British Railways until 1964. Accommodation for passengers on the tour was provided by push-pull set No 608. This

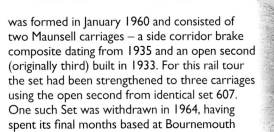

was formed in January 1960 and consisted of two Maunsell carriages – a side corridor brake composite dating from 1935 and an open second (originally third) built in 1933. For this rail tour the set had been strengthened to three carriages using the open second from identical set 607. One such Set was withdrawn in 1964, having spent its final months based at Bournemouth

The Rambling Rose
Rail Tour 23 March 1963

working on the Wareham–Swanage and Brockenhurst – Lymington branches and also the 'old road' to Brockenhurst via Wimborne.

Above: **GRATELEY** 'The last train to Bulford Camp' calls at Grately for a hurried(!) last chance to photograph this location before closure.

Left: **COLEY** During the afternoon the rail tour travelled along the short spur from Southcote Junction, near Reading West station, to Reading Central Goods Yard at Coley. A number of enthusiasts can be seen eagerly exploring this normally inaccessible location. Reading Central Goods Yard was operational from May 1908 until July 1983.

Loco Used   'M7' 30108
Stock used   Push-pull set no. 608

Source of route and timings data:
http://www.sixbellsjunction.co.uk John Clifford (on the train
throughout) Timings (Booked Only) (from John Clifford)

Route :

Loco	Route
30108	Farnborough - Basingstoke - Thorneycrofts Siding (end of former Alton line)
30108	Thorneycrofts Siding (end of former Alton line) - Basingstoke
30108	Basingstoke - Andover Jn - Grateley - Bulford Camp
30108	Bulford Camp - Grateley
30108	Grateley - Salisbury - Salisbury "C" Box
30108	Salisbury "C" Box - Fisherton Goods (former Salisbury GWR station)
30108	Fisherton Goods (former Salisbury GWR station) - Salisbury "C" Box
30108	Salisbury "C" Box - Salisbury - Dean - Romsey - Redbridge - Southampton Central - Eastleigh - Shawford Jn (1) - Winchester City - Basingstoke (Reading line)
30108	Basingstoke (Reading line) - Basingstoke sidings (site of former Basingstoke GWR station)
30108	Basingstoke sidings (site of former Basingstoke GWR station) - Southcote Jn
30108	Southcote Jn - Reading Central
30108	Reading Central - Reading General - Reading Old Jn - Wokingham - Ascot
30108	Ascot - Guildford line
30108	Guildford line - Ascot (Guildford line platform)
30108	Ascot (Guildford line platform) - Frimley - Sturt Lane West Curve - Farnborough

M.C Location	Booked
0.00 Farnborough	09.15d
14.54 Basingstoke	09.38a ~ 09.43d
15.26 Thorneycroft Siding (Worting Road Bridge)	09.53a ~ 10.00d
15.78 Basingstoke	10.10a ~ 10.15d
18.38 Worting Jn	10/20
34.14 Andover Jn	10.43a ~ 10.47d
40.44 Grateley	10/57
.70 Bulford	11.33a ~ 11.43d
57.16 Grateley	12/14 (Reversal
68.05 Salisbury	12.30a ~ 12.40d
68.45 Salisbury (GWR)	12.50a ~ 13.35d
69.05 Salisbury	13/46
85. Romsey	14.17a ~ 14.21d
93.43 Southampton Central	14/38
99.14 Eastleigh	14/52
131.10 Enborne Jn	16/07
132.22 Newbury	16.12a ~ 16.20d
147.49 Coley Branch Jn	?
149.26 Reading General	17/28
155.60 Earley	?
167.23 Ascot (point of Jn)	18/08 (reversal)
177.22 Frimley Jn	18/29
178.34 Farnborough	18.35a

Notes: booked route was Shawford Junc. - Winchester Chesil - Whitchurch
Town - Newbury - Didcot - Reading West - Southcote Jn then as shown
but the train was diverted because of a derailment at Whitchurch Town.

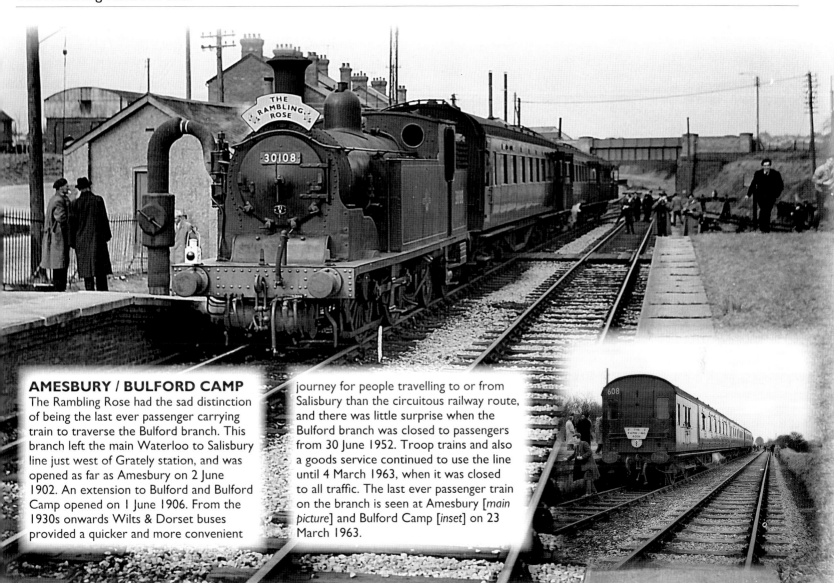

AMESBURY / BULFORD CAMP

The Rambling Rose had the sad distinction of being the last ever passenger carrying train to traverse the Bulford branch. This branch left the main Waterloo to Salisbury line just west of Grately station, and was opened as far as Amesbury on 2 June 1902. An extension to Bulford and Bulford Camp opened on 1 June 1906. From the 1930s onwards Wilts & Dorset buses provided a quicker and more convenient journey for people travelling to or from Salisbury than the circuitous railway route, and there was little surprise when the Bulford branch was closed to passengers from 30 June 1952. Troop trains and also a goods service continued to use the line until 4 March 1963, when it was closed to all traffic. The last ever passenger train on the branch is seen at Amesbury [*main picture*] and Bulford Camp [*inset*] on 23 March 1963.

1963
TV Favourites a selection

World in Action
This hard hitting current affairs programme was first seen in January 1963, and has tackled many controversial topics in succeeding years.

Dr. Who
It was during the early evening of Saturday 23 November 1963 that we watched the first ever episode of Dr. Who, then played by William Hartnell. The Time Lord's ability to regenerate into various human forms has led to a number of actors playing the part over the years, that latest at the time of writing being David Tennant in the 2007/8 series.

Ready, Steady, Go!
Almost compulsory Friday evening viewing for teenagers, this show proclaimed 'The Weekend starts here!'

Younger children enjoyed...
Boss Cat, Deputy Dawg and Fireball XL5.

The Dickie Henderson Show was one of the most popular comedy series of 1963.

Our Man at St. Mark's was a gentle ecclesiastical comedy, starring Leslie Phillips as a young vicar.

The Marriage Lines starred Richard Briers and Prunella Scales as a newly wed young couple.

THE BLUEBELL RAILWAY in 1963

In August 1960 the Bluebell Railway became the first standard gauge line closed by British Railways to be reopened by preservationists, providing the nostalgic delight of haulage by vintage steam locomotives such as the former SE&CR 'Class P' 0-6-0T seen *right*. Until 27 October 1963 the Bluebell Railway was linked to the British Railways network by the electrified branch from Haywards Heath to Horsted Keynes, where the two undertakings shared the station.

Below: **SHEFFIELD PARK** SE&CR 'Class P' 0-6-0T No 323 *Bluebell* pulls into Sheffield Park. This loco was repainted into SE&CR wartime plain green livery, for the 1999 centenary of

the SE&CR. At the time of writing this loco is on static display at the Bluebell Railway awaiting overhaul.

Below: **HORSTED KEYNES** '2HAL' unit No 2624, built in 1939, is ready to depart for Haywards Heath.

Last day of 'the juice'
From Horsted Keynes
to Haywards Heath
Sunday 27 October 1963

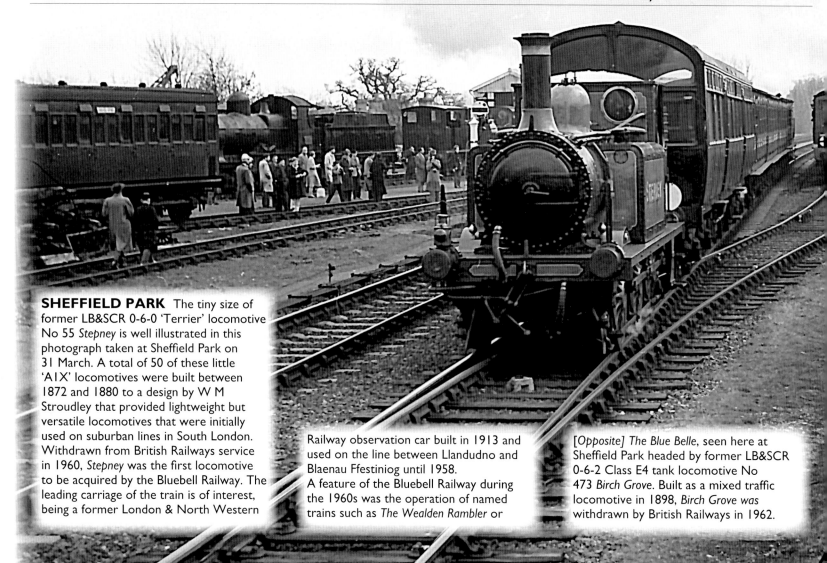

SHEFFIELD PARK The tiny size of former LB&SCR 0-6-0 'Terrier' locomotive No 55 *Stepney* is well illustrated in this photograph taken at Sheffield Park on 31 March. A total of 50 of these little 'A1X' locomotives were built between 1872 and 1880 to a design by W M Stroudley that provided lightweight but versatile locomotives that were initially used on suburban lines in South London. Withdrawn from British Railways service in 1960, *Stepney* was the first locomotive to be acquired by the Bluebell Railway. The leading carriage of the train is of interest, being a former London & North Western

Railway observation car built in 1913 and used on the line between Llandudno and Blaenau Ffestiniog until 1958.
A feature of the Bluebell Railway during the 1960s was the operation of named trains such as *The Wealden Rambler* or

[*Opposite*] *The Blue Belle*, seen here at Sheffield Park headed by former LB&SCR 0-6-2 Class E4 tank locomotive No 473 *Birch Grove*. Built as a mixed traffic locomotive in 1898, *Birch Grove was* withdrawn by British Railways in 1962.

PASSENGERS
ARE STRICTLY
FORBIDDEN TO
CROSS THE LINE

Left: **HORSTED KEYNES** On 27 October 1963 a special train ran from Brighton to Horsted Keynes to mark the last day of public service on the branch from Haywards Heath to Horsted Keynes. Double headed by 'A1X' *Stepney* and 'E4' *Birch Grove* the special is seen nearing Horsted Keynes. The rather elderly carriages were normally used in the Lancing workmen's train.

Inset below: **SHEFFIELD PARK** 4-4-2T locomotive No 8 has an interesting history. Built in 1885 by Neilson and Company of Glasgow for suburban trains on the LSWR, this locomotive was sold to the East Kent Railway after the First World War, but in 1946 was re-purchased by the Southern Railway for £800 and put to work on the branch between Axminster and Lyme Regis until withdrawal by British Railways in 1961.

The crew of No 488 [*below*] are appropriately attired for this fine old locomotive!

Main picture: Former SE&CR 'Class P' 0-6-0T locomotive No 323 *Bluebell* appropriately has charge of the special on the Bluebell Railway's metals. *Bluebell* was one of 8 small locomotives built at

Ashford in 1910 for light passenger work, and was sold to the Bluebell Railway after withdrawal by British Railways in 1960.

SOUTHAMPTON: RMS *Queen Elizabeth* was launched on 27 September 1938, but her fitting out as a luxury liner was delayed because by that time war seemed likely. After more than 18 months laid up she was fitted out for troop transport duties in 1940, a role she was to undertake until October 1945. A year later, on 16 October 1946 RMS *Queen Elizabeth* made her first public trip from Southampton to New York, a route she was to share with her older sister *Queen Mary* throughout her career with Cunard. Ray Ruffell took this photograph of *Queen Elizabeth* at Southampton on 3 September while enjoying a 'View the Liners' cruise around the Docks. It appears that some maintenance work is taking place in readiness for her next sailing across the Atlantic two days later.

The photograph below right shows *Queen Elizabeth* leaving Southampton for New York on 5 September 1963 following the arrival of the *Cunarder* boat train from Waterloo. *Queen Elizabeth* was withdrawn from service in 1968 and became a floating hotel at Everglades in Florida, USA. This venture was not successful, and she was sold for conversion in Hong Kong to become a seagoing mobile university. In January 1972, while this conversion work was being undertaken, fire broke out aboard the liner; she was soon ablaze from end to end and eventually capsized and sank. A sad end for a ship that for many years was the pride of the Cunard fleet

TWIXT RAIL & SEA
Southampton, Portsmouth and the Isle of Wight

Boat trains between London Waterloo and Southampton Docks were still an important operation in 1963. The LSWR had purchased the Southampton Dock Company in 1892, and railway lines to the Old (or Eastern) Docks were laid towards the end of the 19th century. By the mid 1920s there was a demand for additional dock capacity at Southampton, and 400 acres of mudlands near Millbrook were reclaimed to become Southampton New (or Western) Docks which opened in the 1930s; a rail connection to the New Docks via Millbrook opened in June 1935. Bulleid 'West Country Class' Pacific No 34102 *Lapford* is seen after arrival at Southampton New Docks with the *Oriana* boat train on 17 May 1963. *Lapford* entered service in 1950 and was withdrawn in 1967.

PORTSMOUTH AND SOUTHSEA (Low Level) The BR Standard 'Class 5' 4-6-0 was developed from William Stanier's design for the LMS 'black fives'. BR built 172 Standard 'Class 5's during the 1950s, and No 73051 is seen at Portsmouth and Southsea (Low Level) on 4 October in ex works condition including lined green livery. The train will depart at 12.15pm, and at Fareham the three carriages will be attached to the 11.30am train from Brighton and will continue to Plymouth, where arrival will be at 5.59pm.

PORTSMOUTH The crossing from Portsmouth to Ryde is a popular route to the Isle of Wight for foot passengers. On 3 March MV *Shanklin* is departing from Portsmouth Harbour for Ryde. Built by Denny Brothers of Dumbarton, MV *Shanklin* entered service in 1951, and plied between Portsmouth and Ryde until 1980 when she was sold to a preservation society for use as a pleasure steamer. Renamed *Prince Ivanhoe* she struck rocks and sank while cruising off the coast of South Wales the following year; fortunately her passengers were rescued from this perilous situation. In 2008 the ferry service between Portsmouth and Ryde is provided by high speed catamarans.

1963
Happenings (2)

September
Christine Keeler arrested for perjury; Denning Report on Profumo Affair published.
Fylingdales early warning station came into operation.

October
Harold Macmillan resigned as Prime Minister and was succeeded by Sir Alec Douglas-Home.

November
Dartford Tunnel opened.
US President John F Kennedy assassinated; Lyndon B Johnson becomes US President

December
Greek liner *Lakonia* sinks 250 miles west of Gibralter while on a Christmas cruise.

Left: **RYDE PIER HEAD** After crossing by ferry from Portsmouth, the traveller joined the unique Isle of Wight railway network at Ryde Pier Head station, where 'Class 02' 0-4-4T locomotives No 35 *Freshwater* and No 21 *Sandown* are seen [*left*] at the head of their trains on Sunday 19 May 1963. 60 of these sturdy and powerful locomotives were built by the LSWR at Nine Elms between 1889 and 1895, and the type worked all over the LSWR system. Between 1923 and 1949 the Southern Railway transferred 23 of the class to the Isle of Wight, where they were renumbered, and from 1928 onwards given appropriate local names.

No 35 *Freshwater* was built in 1890 and shipped to the Isle of Wight in 1949 while No 21 *Sandown* was built in 1891 and transferred to the island in 1924; both locomotives were withdrawn in 1966.

The coaching stock on the Isle of Wight was also of pre-grouping origin, and delightfully antique by the early 1960s. A few minutes after the first photograph, No 21 leads a Ventnor bound train consisting of a mixture of former SE&CR and LB&SCR carriages, along the pier towards Ryde Esplanade station.

Right: **VENTNOR** The end of the line at Ventnor was photographed on 12 April 1963; 'Class O2' No 28 *Ashey* is being topped up with water after arrival with a train from Ryde. *Ashey* was built in 1890, transferred to the Isle of Wight in 1926 and withdrawn in 1966. Sadly the attractive terminus at Ventnor was closed

from 18 April 1966 when the line from Ryde was truncated at Shanklin.

In 2008 an authentic taste of the island railways as they were in days gone by is available by taking a trip on the Isle of Wight Steam Railway between Smallbrook Junction and Wooton, while the line from Ryde to Shanklin has an interest of its own, being operated by ex London Transport 1938 tube stock.

YEOVIL TOWN Locomotive Depot
was adjacent to Yeovil Town Station, reached
by a short branch from Yeovil Junction on
the Waterloo – Exeter line and also the first
intermediate station on the branch from Yeovil
Pen Mill to Taunton. The original negative for
this illustration has unfortunately deteriorated
over the years but has been included as
a varied selection of motive power was
photographed at the depot on 3 April. On the
far left we see Bulleid West Country Pacific No
34007 *Wadebridge*. New in 1945 *Wadebridge*
had just over two years left in service before
withdrawal in October 1965. The three
locomotives in front of the shed are (left) BR
Standard 'Class 4' 2-6-0 No 76067 dating from
the early 1950s, (centre) 'Class U' 2-6-0 No
31637 which was built by the Southern Railway
at Ashford Works in 1931 and withdrawn
later in 1963 and (right) 0-6-0 Pannier Tank
No 9732 representing the Western Region.
Notice also the small crane just to the left of
the shed building. The slightly bucolic nature of
this nonetheless busy shed is nicely captured in
the photograph, but sadly this interesting scene
was soon to be no more, as Yeovil Town
Depot was closed in 1965.

Bottom right: **DERBY** In many ways the main interest in this photograph taken at Derby is not the Ivatt 2-6-0 No 46502 on the parcels train, but the two diesel locomotives visible in the background. The diesel on the left was one of three prototypes built at BR Ashford Works in Kent to a design by former Southern Railway CME Oliver Bulleid, although the locomotive did not appear in service until 1951. Numbered 10201, 10202 and 10203 they were designated '1Co-Co1' all three were withdrawn during 1963 and broken up at Cashmores, Great Bridge in 1968. The diesel on the right No 10000 is a slightly older machine that was built at Derby Works as a prototype for the LMS in 1947. After 1955 both the locomotives seen here were working on the London Midland Region, but in the early 1960s, with large numbers of production diesel locomotives entering service, the prototypes

1963
LOCOS ON SHED

were becoming oddities. By early 1963 the two examples seen here were stored out of use at Derby, although they were not officially withdrawn from service until December.

1963
No 1 Records

January
Bachelor Boy	*Cliff Richard*
Dance on	*Shadows*
Diamonds	*Jet Harris & Tony Meehan*

February
Wayward Wind — *Frank Ifield*

March
| Summer Holiday | *Cliff Richard* |
| Foot tapper | *Shadows* |

April
How do you do it? — *Gerry & The Pacemakers*

May
From me to you — *Beatles*

June
I like it — *Gerry & The Pacemakers*

July
Confessing that I love you — *Frank Ifield*

August
Devil in disguise	*Elvis Presley*
Sweets for my sweet	*Searchers*
Bad to me	*Billy J Kramer & The Dakotas*

September
She loves you — *Beatles*

October
Do you love me? — *Brian Poole & The Tremeloes*

November
You'll never walk alone — *Gerry & The Pacemakers*

December
I want to hold your hand — *Beatles*

NINE ELMS Nine Elms had been the principal locomotive depot of the LSWR, and occupied an extensive site in Battersea beside the main line out of Waterloo. A notable feature was the massive locomotive coaling plant, which dated from 1923 and was built largely of concrete. The imposing structure can be seen in the background of this photograph, taken on 20 August. Loaded coal wagons were hoisted to the top, where they were tipped to empty their contents into the hopper below.

Locomotive tenders were then coaled by gravity from this hopper. In the foreground of this evocative view we see two rebuilt Bulleid Light Pacifics. Closest to the camera is 'Battle of Britain Class' No 34058 *Sir Frederick Pile* which was new in 1947, rebuilt in 1960 and withdrawn from BR service in 1964. Over 20 years later this locomotive was rescued from a South Wales scrap yard for restoration by the Avon Valley Railway near Bristol. Beyond *Sir Frederick Pile* is 'West Country Class' No 34044

Wollacombe. This locomotive was new in 1946, rebuilt in 1960 and remained in service almost until the end of steam traction on the Southern Region, being withdrawn in May 1967. Nine Elms Shed was closed in 1967; the site was cleared and subsequently became the New Covent Garden vegetable and fruit market, which in turn allowed the original Covent Garden market site in Central London to become the trendy and vibrant area we know 40 years later in 2007.

REDHILL These photographs were taken on the bitterly cold morning of 8 January.

Above: That day motive power for the 6.50am train from Reading to Redhill was provided by ex Great Western 4-6-0 No 7817 *Garsington Manor*. The Great Western Railway built 20 of these 'Manor' Class locomotives in 1938-9 and a further 10 were built under British Railways auspices in 1950. *Garsington Manor*, after which this locomotive is named, is near Oxford. A Tudor building, it was from 1914 until 1928 the home of Lady Ottoline Morrell, and was much frequented by other members of the Bloomsbury Group, including Aldous Huxley, Lytton Strachey and Bertrand Russell.

Right: The photograph on the right captures the raw atmosphere as the leading fitter, carrying a kettle, takes a break to go and make some tea. Where the snow has been packed down into ice walking would have been quite treacherous, but smoke is rising in a homely way from the chimney of the stove in the converted carriage on the left. Notice that the snow has melted from the roof of this section of the carriage, but remains on the roof of the former brake section at the far end.

Opposite: **REDHILL** A familiar piece of railway equipment in steam days, the turntable has been rendered superfluous by conversion to electric or diesel power. The turntable at Redhill is shown on 8 January. 'Class U' 2-6-0 No 31627 is being turned after arrival with a passenger train from Reading. Built at the Southern Railway Ashford Works in 1929, this locomotive remained in service until 1965. Notice that at least two of the trucks in the sidings are condemned.

Below: **SEATON JUNCTION** One way of eliminating the need to turn a steam locomotive was to operate push-pull or auto trains, an expedient that was to be found on many branch lines. West of Salisbury, the former Southern main line from Waterloo to Exeter and its branches came under Western Region control from 1 January 1963. The new regime lost no time in replacing the former Southern Railway push-pull carriages that were used on the branch from Seaton Junction to Seaton with more modern auto-trailers. Coach W238W is seen at Seaton Junction on 15 April; despite its non-standard design this carriage was built as late as 1954. The Seaton

branch was closed in March 1966, although the track bed between Colyton and Seaton is now the home of the delightful Seaton Tramway.

Below: **REDHILL** The satisfaction of a good job well done – a preparation and disposal crew on shed with 'Class U' 2-6-0 No 31638.

Index

Acknowledgements

It would not have been possible to produce this book without the use of the wonderful collection of photographs taken by the late Ray Ruffell; virtually all of the illustrations in this volume started in his camera.

Ray was a railwayman by profession, but his interest in transport went far beyond his day to day work. In his off duty time Ray travelled widely throughout the British Isles and in so doing created an extensive photographic record of the railway system during a period when great changes were underway. Many scenes that were everyday and commonplace when Ray photographed them have now been swept away for ever and the memories he has captured on film, precious at the time, are now beyond price. It is pleasing to record that this huge collection of photographs has been kept complete and is now in the safe keeping of *The NOSTALGIA Collection*, forming an important part of their photographic archives.

I would like to say a sincere thank you to the team at *The NOSTALGIA Collection* for inviting me to write this book, which I hope is a worthy member of the Railways and Recollections series. The cheerful and willing help I have received from Peter Townsend, Will Adams, Mick Sanders and David Walshaw has been warmly appreciated and I feel deeply honoured to work with such kind people.

Ray Ruffell The final photograph (left) shows Ray Ruffell on duty on the Southern Region of British Railways in 1963, standing beside the footplate of Bulleid 'West Country' Pacific locomotive No 34091 *Weymouth*. This locomotive entered service in 1949 and was officially named at Weymouth station on 29 December that year by the Mayor of Weymouth and Melcombe Regis, Alderman Alfred Percy Burt. No 34091 was withdrawn from service in 1964.

I hope you have enjoyed this look back at 1963 and that you will wish to sample more years in the Railways and Recollections series.